SEX
LOVE
RELIGION

Larry Oakner

BLIND tAttoo PRESS

©2018 Larry Oakner
ISBN #978-0-692-11495-7

www.blindtattoopress.org

Cover design by Saara Untracht-Oakner

For all those I loved and love

Acknowledgements

The following poems appeared in these publications:

The Tattered Talis
Jewish Literary Journal

Golem
Kerem

The Sciences of Love
PROKVR.COM

And then, Zen
Lost Coast Review

Pride in Humility
The Shambhala Times

My Mother in a Red Hat
Home Planet News Online

Maitreya
The Buddhist Review

Desire

The night is a forest of sighs.
Between the trees there are whispers of longing.
No one but the beautiful can understand what is being said.
There are these stars that come down to earth as women,
more lovely than the purest strand of pearls.
When they arrive, they take only the clouds full of moon
for their clothes.
Only they can hear the deep, slumberous breath
of the leaves who dream about the night sky
and the absence of certain stars.

Marriage vows

We are a balance tipping in a breeze.
　We are a bridge spanning river banks.
Like sky and sea we make the horizon.
　Our time is both midnight and noon.
Suns and planets will orbit us.
　Words are spoken.
We are bonded by hearts and days.

The Tattered Talis

For Rabbi Batsheva Meiri

My grandfather's talis
is yellowed as a page from his old siddur,
the silver collar stained by the history of his life:
these were tears for the family left behind,
that was salt sprayed from prayers at sea,
this was sweat wiped from a six-day week.
Here his lips kissed the corners of the shawl.
From him to my father,
the threads tie generations together.

My father's talis
is creased as the pages in a Haggadah,
the embroidery ruined by the rub of his life:
these were drops from kiddush wine,
that was ink from the fountain pen,
this lipstick from a wedding kiss.
Here he snagged tzitzis in the zippered bag.

From my father to me,
the threads tie generations together.
My talis is tattered as a Sunday school bible,
the fabric unraveled by the pull of my life:
these were the holes eaten by moths,
that was from something that spilled,
this rip from a time I don't remember.
Here it was crushed in a drawer.

We spend our days untangling all that we inherit,
in the hope that we can find the end
to reweave our lives into whole cloth from a common
thread and tie loose strings into sacred knots
like a talis of brilliant white.

The Rose of Sharon

The Rose of Sharon isn't really a rose,
but it's still a flower as real as the name
you whispered in my ear in a voice
rubbed smooth by a thousand hours of midnight and smoke.
The space between real and imagined
is a close as your breath on my cheek.
What is real are your eyes that burn as blue as gas flame
and all that I imagine when I close my own.
The memory of your breasts,
like "the ghost of a rose under dew"
haunts me for months.
This is real:
If I could touch the milk of your skin,
luminous under blacklight,
it would real as my own.
The fire of your hair enflames my mind
where what is real becomes hotter because it is not
and where the Rose of Sharon blooms
over and over and over.

A pound of lychees

For Saara

Passing through town on tour
my daughter calls me with a craving for fresh lychees
so we head down to Chinatown,
strolling past renovated tenements,
and share a bag of the succulent floral fruit.
Fingers sticky with juice, we toss the husks into the gutter
just as a summer thunderstorm rolls in.
We duck into a deserted bar to dodge the drenching rain
and over drinks we swap iPhone photos of her last gig.
This is the tempo of her times now:
Hugging her is Heisenberg's uncertainty,
Love measured in quantum moments,
her rhythm propelling her forward
even as I try to hold onto the woman she is becoming.

Golem

1
I heard this story was true
how Rabbi Levi of Prague
took on the old lie: the Blood Libel,
thrown against the ghetto walls like red paint.
And when the lie had taken on a life of its own
enough to bring death into the shtetl,
the Rebbe climbed the wooden ladder,
like the angels in Jacob's dream,
ascending to the old synagogue attic
where amidst clouds of cobwebs and soot
he gathered dust with his hands and,
shaping the form of a man on the floor,
the Rabbi thumbnailed truth on the golem's brow
and the mannequin glowed with a plutonian half-life.

2
Every day I see a thousand golems
sleep walking, dumb as death
the truth written across their brows
where they can only see it on someone else.
There are truths to wake up to every day
if you know where to look:
The truth of my daughter patting
my leg as we sit together.
Truth is as small as a sparrow that appeared
in my son's bedroom, darting back and forth
before gathering the courage to fly out the open window.

If the difference between truth and death is life
then it is in my father's polished redwood casket
where I tucked my mother's goodbye note,
and, as well, in the miracle of her remission,
hair returning, luxuriant and silver.
Every morning I face the truth in my spit and image.
After someone dies, we cover the mirrors.

3
After the golem had dumbly done its job,
the Rabbi rubbed out its life:
The difference between truth and death
is only a letter with no sound of its own
except the sound of the breath
which is life itself and the first flaming letter
of the seventy secret names of God.

Imagining you

By candlelight two garnets
illuminate the blush of your nape
where my lips belong.
Your open collar deepens
a shadow of an invitation.
Wood smoke mingles
with your fragrance.
Memory intoxicates me.

The red truck

For Jesse

You saw
a Chevy pickup pulled over
to the side of the country road under a tree,
the passenger door open
and a field on the edge of the frame.

I pictured
the same argument over his lost job,
his drinking, her mother and
the young wife flinging open the door
and jumping out as he jams on the brakes
to pull over on the wrong-ass side of the road
to chase her across the field.

You tell stories with your eyes
and made me see
the winking now between then and next
where a red truck is parked
under a tree on the shoulder of a back road
with one door and a story open forever.

When the heart opens like a window

On a business trip to Bangkok,
I am a stranger in a strange land
Visiting the Temple of the Emerald Buddha.
Taking the lead of my guide
I remove my shoes and join the push of worshippers, tourists,
day-trippers past the guardian demons into the hall
to pay my respects to the tiny jade statue
high on his golden podium wrapped in his little kingly robe.
I watch the others and then kneel low and bow,
touching my forehead to the immaculate floor.
Without warning, tears well up
and joy splashes over me.
Compassion becomes a passing companion:
the Buddha smiles on me.
As I leave, an old orange-wrapped monk
hands me a banana.
So I eat it.

The Sciences of Love

Chemistry

What is flammable about us ignites passions
that conflagrate into both love and strife.
You are the arsonist of my heart,
setting me ablaze with your spark.
After all the years, you still light my fire.

Astronomy

My tongue connects
the constellation of freckles on your body,
swirling around the galaxy of your sex:
You quiver.

Geography

At night on her side
her hips rise like Californian coastal mountains.
Her body rolls in dark round waves
I sail the crests over her.
Tossing stars, she drowns me.

Salvation

You wrest me from my dark
     with the spark of your Yankee wit
You thaw me from my chill
     with the warmth of your giving heart
You breeze me from my doldrums
     with the tickle of your laughter
You bridge my longing for you
     with the span of your ruddy passion
that stretches across years

Shopping in Kennebunkport

What caught my eye
in the Asian antique shop with the Going Out Of
Business sign was a faded green *furoshiki*,
a simple Japanese cotton cloth
for wrapping purchases, printed with *sumi* characters
and a traditional *enso* circling them all.
Unwrapping the meaning of the image
I found that in a garden of Ryoan-ji temple
there is a stone water basin
where water continually flows
to purify our hands that touch our lives
and our mouth that sanctifies our words
and carved around the stone surface
are four characters that mean nothing alone
  ware, tada taru (wo) shiru
but with the center water-filled square
the empty opening unites them all to say
"You already have everything you need."

Going down

I called her pussy Little Scarlet
for it was as red and sticky sweet
as English strawberry preserves.
But that patch of ruby tangle is long gone,
her memory overgrown by seasons passed.
But O how delicious she was!

Heartbreak

When a heart breaks
does it make a sound like
a spoon cracking a soft-boiled eggshell
or a sob coming from a crouch
in the corner of a bathroom
a slam of a car door
as it pulls away from a bus bench
or the silence of a swipe across
the Delete button
is it a jangle of keys
tossed on a table
the click of a latch closing
the tiny plunk of a ring
thrown into the ocean
or is it the last word
you will ever remember?

And then, Zen

1. Sitting still
The exquisite pain—
Doing zazen the first time.
Spotted cat stretching.

2. There's no denying it
A wild fox trots along the median strip pausing
to glance beyond his brushy tail.
He pants through his thin black lips
while traffic whizzes by—oblivious.
Am I the fox? Is the fox me?
A monk was condemned to live
five hundred lifetimes as a fox
for asking the wrong question
until he was released in a word:
Ignore karma and embrace it.

3. The measure of emptiness
The beaten bowl of blackened copper
clad inside with purest gold—
Which holds more value,
the vessel or the void?

Invisibility

Men reach a point in their lives when,
whether blinded by the reflection
off thinning silver hair
or disguised by the shadows under eyes
or camouflaged by the sag of muscles gone soft with age,
we become invisible
in the radiance of young women's beauty.
Along the streets and beach,
they cannot see us for who we are or were:
They don't see the proud acuteness of a hard-on,
feel the talented tongue or the caress of strong hands,
imagine the gymnastics and the embrace of afterglow.
To them, we are faceless fathers, anonymous uncles,
clerks, clergy, manikins—dickless, all.
They cannot feel our palpable ache of lust,
the gut punch, the arrhythmic skip
every time we see the flawless skin
of their summered backs, or rounded breasts promising
pneumatic bliss, the intelligent glint in their eyes,
the flash of their smiles,
legs that can support the wildest dreams,
or an ass that can snap a neck back over a shoulder.
Yet if we stare too long
we pierce the veil of invisibility
and we become pervert, creep, asshole
when all we long for is to be seen
as the sexual beings we once were
or could be if only.

History

Remember the Valentine's bouquet
of Florentine flowers I once bought you
from the cool shade
of a Quattrocento palazzo?
What lasts long after blossoms compost
is a love that does not fade.

Pride in Humility

In the kitchen of the Zen monastery
I am assigned to the work practice I asked for.
But the cook wordlessly instructs me
to clean and prep a huge carton of romaine.
Me! With forty years of chef's skills
reduced to pantry duty!
Me! Who should be chopping
the main course of vegetables for dinner!
Working with a young woman
we silently wash the leaves in a water bath,
prune the rotting blotches,
dry the leaves in a spinner
with a crank of the heavy handle,
lay out the greens on a towel,
then tear them into bite size pieces.
Wash, prune, spin, dry, tear
Wash, prune, spin, dry, tear
Wash prune spin dry tear
Washprunespindrytear
until my mind is as empty as the carton.
A lettuce leaf humbles me.

False alarm

You are working the night shift
like a fireman dozing
boots and turnout coat standing in place
      ready
for the 3 am call
that may never come
but ready nonetheless

There will be no fire tonight
or any night for that matter
no frayed wires smoldering
no spark catching curtains
or passion inflamed to the flash point
      between us
So you can close your eyes and dream

My mother in a red hat

She is sitting serenely on a sofa
in the salon of a friend's motor yacht
wearing her pea coat and a rolled brim cotton hat
looking into the camera
somewhere between Ketchikan and bemusement.

A guested passenger, she travels widowed
across the water my father always feared.
This voyage, a few years after his sudden death,
even as her cancer was eating her lung,
was simply another trip on her life's late itinerary.

What was she thinking when that photo
caught her trademark crooked smile?
Had she renounced her trepidations,
bid a grand slam now with nothing left to lose,
after a life spent following the same recipes?

I had seen that look before
when she shared a secret
said everything without uttering a word
or when she confided
she wanted balloons released at her funeral
which led me to ask if the metastasis
had short-circuited her brain
  and then that smile again.
Even when she endured radiation therapy
head clapt in a stereostatic frame,
there was that enigmatic Mona Lisa in a Polaroid.
24

So when the yacht anchored off some unnamed rivulet
that emptied into a cove where grizzlies
come to feast on spawning salmon,
the bunch of seventy-year olds piled into the Zodiac
and the captain cranked the throttle wide open
plowing the raft ahead
while my mother stood in the bucking prow
gripping the bowline like a rodeo rider,
her hat blown back.

The Bodhisattva Quartet

Avalokitesvara
It's not about me
but about the tiny spider cradled outside
the birdseed scattered in the frozen snow
the child's cleft lip made whole
the frail old man who got down the steps.
Everyone suffers
but when compassion is given
from a self that's given away
it's about all living things.

Manjushri
I've been an ignoramus
more times than I care to realize
said the wrong things
missed her point
didn't get it.
But if you cut through the crap
and slash away the BS
there are those flashing moments
when wisdom is what's left over
and I am left holding
the most perfectly transcendent flower
risen from the dumb muck.

Samantabhadra
 Some times are harder
the nose runs
drool pools
posture wilts
the mind busies itself
with dim histories and plans.
Then there are mornings
the slow metronome of breaths
the half-closed gaze
the blank awareness:
Perfect.
Why do you think it's called practice?

Matreiya
 Just you wait
one day in about 8,000 years
when the Truth is forgotten
he'll come around
and make it all right.
Funny thing about the future,
it's not about hope
which is what you want to happen
it's not about worry
which is what you don't
it's what the sign in the dive bar always says
"Free beer tomorrow."

El tiempo vuela

Meditating between the shush of the Pacific's crashing surf
and the bonging bells of Prime from our Lady of
Guadalupe, I'm vacationing again in Puerto Vallarta.

Ten years we've been coming here,
first as part of the tourist trade that ebbs and flows
like the tides along the Malecón.

But by now I recognize the stores and nightspots
that have opened and shuttered, know my way
up and down the cobblestoned *calles* and *avenidas*

where I can glance into the townspeople's meager rooms,
the clutter of toys, old furniture, the lights low, the TV on
and the *abuela* watching me, sleepy-eyed, as I pass by like time.

This trip, we charter a boat to motor us down the coast,
lazily following the bay, twin Yamahas cutting through the
ocean, the beloved ocean of my youth, though my birthplace
miles north.

Suddenly, a humpback whale rises to spout 25 yards off
starboard. It blows, catches a breath and gently arches
under with a wave of its flukes.
  "This is the warm season when they come to find a
  mate and calve," the captain says.

We're trolling lines when we get a hit and I reel in a
Spanish mackerel, silver with yellow stripes, sharp
teeth, spraying blood on the deck.

Within an hour we're eating it freshly grilled at a
restaurant on the beach at Yelapa.

I've been thinking about compassion lately, the results
of my zazen: holding back judgments, the quick quip,
trying to shift my point of view to the Other, and
consider what it must feel like to be hooked when
struggling just to stay alive.

These are my big questions now, the horizon far off
but noted, prompted by the expectation of my first
grandchild, the early deaths of friends and what I
intend to do with the rest of my days.

But today, I'm in PV, gallery walking, and I find an
elegant sculpture of the Buddha's head, almost art
deco glazed in celadon, so incongruous yet enticing
amidst the native art that I want to take it home.

Days later, we tour the San Miguel Arcángel Parish in
Pitallal, where the Risen Christ, carved from a single
massive 26-foot tree trunk, floats magically over the
altar, faintly smiling;

Jesus presenting the mudras for reassurance and charity
on Ash Wednesday and over the Blessing of the Mariachi
who, in gratitude, play a medley of classic show tunes.

Religion has always been society's palliative,
the ritual reassurances that there is something beyond,
(though I am partial to ee cummings' uncle's worm farm.)

Regardless of the faith, I reduce all their lessons
to living my life each day: Don't be an asshole, do your
best, be kind to people and animals. What more is there?

We are all really just tourists here, riding a rickety bus
packed with children, families and old people over a
rough road while a crazy kid in the back seat
sings a song and beats time on his drum.

Larry Oakner's poems have followed the trajectory of his life's search for the Middle Path, traveling between the sacred and the profane. Oakner's poems have appeared in The Intima: A Journal of Narrative Medicine, Tricycle: Buddhist News, PROVOKR.com, The Shambhala Times, The Jewish Literary Review, Lost Coast Review, Home Planet News, Mystic Nebula, Mobius, Long Island Quarterly, CCAR Journal, Kerem and SPSM&H. He is also the author of a chapbook, *Sitting Still,* and his essays on poets Jack Spicer and William Carlos Williams appeared in Manroot and Thoth: Graduate Studies in English (Syracuse University), respectively. Oakner received his Master's Degree in Creative Writing from UCLA.